True Stories From Ancient China

Science and Scientists

By Zhu Kang

Illustrated by Hong Tao and Feng Congying

LONG RIVER PRESS
San Francisco

Copyright © 2005 Long River Press

Published in the United States of America by

LONG RIVER PRESS
360 Swift Avenue, Suite 48
South San Francisco, CA 94080
www.longriverpress.com

In association with Dolphin Books

Editor: Luo Tianyou

No part of this book may be reproduced without written permission of the Publisher.

ISBN 1-59265-038-4

Library of Congress Control Number: 2004113548

Printed in China

10 9 8 7 6 5 4 3 2 1

ZHANG HENG AND ASTRONOMY

张衡与天文学

IN ANCIENT CHINA THERE WERE THREE THEORIES ABOUT THE RELATIONSHIP OF THE EARTH, THE SKY, AND THE UNIVERSE…

THE SKY IS LIKE A ROUND CANOPY WHICH REVOLVES ONE WAY, AND THE SUN, MOON, AND STARS REVOLVE IN THE OPPOSITE DIRECTION.

THE EARTH IS SQUARE WITH EACH SIDE COMPRISING 250,000 SQUARE MILES.

THE SKY HAS NO SHAPE AND THE SUN, MOON, AND STARS ALL FLOAT.

THE SKY IS LIKE AN EGG SHELL AND THE EARTH THE YOLK. THEY FLOAT ABOUT THE AIR AND REVOLVE CONSTANTLY.

ZHANG HENG (78-139 A.D.) WAS A FAMOUS ASTONOMER OF ANCIENT CHINA DURING THE EASTERN HAN DYNASTY. ZHANG INVENTED THE ARMILLARY SPHERE, AN ANCIENT MODEL OF THE HEAVENS. HE ALSO INVENTED THE SEISMOGRAPH AND WAS THE FIRST TO DISCOVER THE CAUSES OF LUNAR ECLIPSES.

All these theories seem reasonable, but which one is correct?

The stars move, but their movement is not random.

Master, it's late. Have some tea.

Can't you see I'm looking at stars?

Do people believe the sky is an upside down bowl?

It's one theory.

Master, the stars are innumerable!

I have counted 2,500 so far.

It would be easy to count them if people could hold the sky in their hands.

I agree.

3

4

IN 117 A.D., ZHANG HENG COMPLETED THE FIRST BRONZE CELESTIAL GLOBE, KNOWN AS AN ARMILLARY SPHERE. ITS MOTION WAS GENERATED BY WATER, AND IT WAS USED TO SHOW THE MOTION OF THE SUN, MOON, AND STARS.

Your Majesty, the circumference of the armillary sphere is 16 feet. It is divided into 365.25 degrees. It rotates from this year's Winter Solstice to the next. Each rotation cycle is one year.

HERE IS HOW THE MOVEMENT OF THE SPHERE WAS RECORDED IN AN ANCIENT TEXT. ZHANG HENG USED THE FORCE OF DRIPPING WATER TO MOVE THE SPHERE SLOWLY WHILE DEMONSTRATING THE WAXING AND WANING OF THE MOON.

The revolving armillary sphere demonstrates the celestial phenomena of the four seasons and the twelve two-hour periods in the day.

What makes it turn?

The dripping water moves the big wheel, which in turn drives the smaller wheel. In this way the sphere can be made to rotate slowly.

Fascinating. How does it work?

I see. The stars in the sky correspond to the points on the surface of the sphere.

AFTER YEARS OF RESEARCH AND OBSERVATION, ZHANG HENG WROTE *LING XIAN* (THE SPIRITUAL CONSTITUTION OF THE UNIVERSE), AND *HUN TIAN YI TU ZHU* (THE DIAGRAMS OF THE ARMILLARY SPHERE). ALTHOUGH HE IS KNOWN AS ONE OF ANCIENT CHINA'S GREATEST ASTRONOMERS, HIS CONTRIBUTION TO CHINESE SCIENCE CONTINUED TO GROW AND DEVELOP.

ZHANG HENG AND HIS FAMILY WERE RELAXING ONE DAY, WHEN SUDDENLY…

Oh no! An earthquake!

It's so terrible!

Hurry!

I wonder where it took place?

I'm scared, Dad!

BETWEEN 92 AND 125 A.D., ZHANG HENG CATALOGED 26 STRONG EARTHQUAKES. HE RECORDED THE CONDITIONS AND CHARACTERISTICS OF EACH EARTHQUAKE. YET, HE COULD NOT PINPOINT THEIR LOCATION, OR EPICENTER.

8

Now. Each dragon faces east, south, west, north, northwest, southwest, northeast, and southeast. The bronze balls in the dragon's mouth are sensitive to seismic movement. Wherever the earthquake is taking place, it will cause the ball facing in that direction to fall into the frog's mouth.

Father, it's brilliant!

Let me try!

I'm so tired!

Ha Ha! You're not as strong as the earth!

10

WHILE NO INNER MECHANISM OF ZHANG HENG'S SEISMOGRAPH SURVIVES, HISTORICAL RECORDS SHOW THE STRUCTURE ADHERING TO THESE FUNDAMENTAL PRINCIPLES:

A HEAVY STICK STANDS IN THE CENTER OF THE SEISMOGRAPH. THE UPPER DIAMETER OF THE STICK IS THICKER THAN ITS DIAMETER AT THE BASE.

A FORCE TRANSMITTED TO THE BASE OF THE STICK IS MAGNIFIED ONCE IT REACHES THE TOP, CAUSING THE STICK TO FALL IN THE DIRECTION WHERE THE FORCE ORIGINATES.

THE FALLEN STICK THUS HITS A ROD WHICH OPENS THE DRAGON'S MOUTH AND CAUSES THE BALL TO FALL OUT.

ZHANG HENG LIVED TO THE AGE OF 62. HE MADE MANY OUTSTANDING CONTRIBUTIONS TO THE FIELD OF CHINESE SCIENCE.

HERE IS A BRONZE WEATHER-VANE IN THE SHAPE OF A BIRD. ITS HEAD ALWAYS POINTS INTO THE WIND AND ITS BODY REVOLVES IN ACCORDANCE WITH THE WIND'S DIRECTION. THIS IS THE EARLIEST KNOWN WEATHER-VANE IN CHINESE HISTORY.

ZHANG HENG MADE A DRUM CART FOR MEASURING DISTANCE BASED ON THE PRINCIPLE OF GEARS. FOR EVERY LI (OR 1/3 MILE) THE CART TRAVELS, THE WOODEN FIGURINE WILL BEAT THE DRUM ONCE.

ZHANG HENG ALSO EXCELLED IN ARITHMETIC AND CALCULATED THE VALUE OF π AS 3.1622.

ZHANG HENG WAS ALSO A WELL KNOWN WRITER. HIS WORKS, *ODE TO THE TWO CAPITALS*, *ODE TO THE TILLERS*, AND *FOUR LAMENTS*, WERE HIGHLY ACCLAIMED IN THE LITERARY CIRCLES OF ANCIENT CHINA.

ZHANG HENG WAS ALSO ONE OF THE FOUR GREAT PAINTERS OF THE EASTERN HAN.

HIS TOMB IS LOCATED IN HIS HOME TOWN OF NANYANG, HENAN PROVINCE.

ZU CHONGZHI AND THE VALUE OF π

祖冲之与圆周率

ZU CHONGZHI'S GRANDFATHER WAS AN IMPERIAL OFFICIAL IN CHARGE OF ENGINEERING. HE OFTEN WENT TO INSPECT CONSTRUCTION SITES.

Father, don't overwork yourself.

I'll be fine.

Grandpa! It's too stuffy in here!

What? Chongzhi! Is that you?

ZU CHONGZHI (429-500 A.D.) WAS A SCIENTIST OF THE SOUTHERN DYNASTIES PERIOD. ZHU DETERMINED THAT THE REAL VALUE OF π (PI, OR, THE RATIO OF THE CIRCUMFERENCE OF A CIRCLE TO ITS DIAMETER) LAY BETWEEN TWO NUMBERS, 3.1415926, AND 3.1415927. HE ALSO GAVE TWO FRACTIONAL VALUES FOR π: AN "INACCURATE" VALUE OF 22/7, AND AN "ACCURATE" VALUE OF 355/113. ZU ALSO EXCELLED IN ASTRONOMY AND INVENTED THE *DA MING* CALENDAR.

THE BOOK WAS *LING XIAN* (THE SPIRITUAL CONSTITUTION OF THE UNIVERSITY) WRITTEN BY NONE OTHER THAN ZHANG HENG (NOTED ASTRONOMER OF THE EASTERN HAN DYNASTY). ZU CHONGZHI READ IT WITH GREAT INTEREST, AND SUDDENLY A NEW WORLD OPENED BEFORE HIM.

ONCE ZU'S GRANDFATHER REALIZED HOW INFATUATED HIS GRANDSON WAS WITH ASTRONOMY, HE TOOK HIM TO VISIT THE GREAT SCHOLAR HE CHENGTIAN.

15

FROM THAT TIME FORWARD, ZU CHONGZHI BECAME THE DISCIPLE OF HE CHENGTIAN. TOGETHER WITH HIS TEACHER, ZU OBSERVED THE HEAVENLY BODIES AND MADE DETAILED OBSERVATIONS, THEREBY MAKING A SYSTEMATIC STUDY OF ASTRONOMY, THE CALENDAR, AND LAWS OF MOTION. HE CHENGTIAN WOULD LATER PUBLISH THE *YUANJIA* CALENDAR, WHICH WAS WIDELY USED THROGHOUT THE EMPIRE.

AT THE AGE OF 25, ZU ENTERED THE HUALIN ACADEMY, AN IMPERIAL INSTITUTE FOR ADVANCED LEARNING.

ON SEPTEMBER 15TH IN THE YEAR 459 A.D., ZU PREDICTED A LUNAR ECLIPSE.

The Yuanjia Calendar does not show an eclipse.

The moon is so bright.

How can that be?

Zu must be crazy.

AS A TOOL USED FOR COUNTING, THE ABACUS HAD NOT YET BEEN INVENTED. INSTEAD, ZU USED SMALL STICKS TO CALCULATE CELESTIAL PHENOMENA.

十九年七閏改為三百九十一年

一百四十四閏歲差每四十五年

為往西移一度 回帰年

為三六五点二四二

八一八一四八一日

亥点月為二七点

二二三三三日；水星会合

周期為一百一十五点八八日金星

会合周期為五百八十三点九三日。

IN THE YEAR 462, ZU COMPLETED THE *DA MING* CALENDAR, WHICH GREATLY IMPROVED THE ACCURACY OF MEASURING THE LENGTH OF THE LUNAR YEAR.

I will create a new calendar.

17

EMPEROR XIAOWU CALLED IN THE MINISTERS TO DISCUSS ZU'S NEW *DA MING* CALENDAR.

IN 464 A.D. EMPEROR XIAOWU DIED AND THE ADOPTION OF THE DAMING CALENDAR WAS LAID ASIDE. ZU WAS DISMISSED FROM HIS POST AND WENT HOME.

IN ANCIENT CHINA THERE WAS A THEORY THAT IF THE DIAMATER OF THE CIRCLE WAS 1, THE CIRCUMFERENCE WAS 3, BUT THIS THEORY WAS INCORRECT.

IN ORDER TO MEET THE NEEDS OF CONSTRUCTION ENGINEERING, MACHINE BUILDING, WEIGHT AND MEASURES, CALENDAR MAKING, AND ASTRONOMY AND SCIENCE, ANCIENT MATHEMATICIANS GAVE THEIR OWN VALUES FOR π:

LIU XIN OF THE WESTERN HAN DYNASTY

ZHANG HENG OF THE EASTERN HAN DYNASTY.

IN THE LATE 3RD CENTURY, LIU HUI, A MATHEMATICIAN, CALCULATED π BY CUTTING THE AREA OF A CIRCLE INTO SEGMENTS.

Master Liu, you've been watching me cutting these stones. What have you learned?

A lot, actually.

Let me measure it. The circumference is three times the diameter.

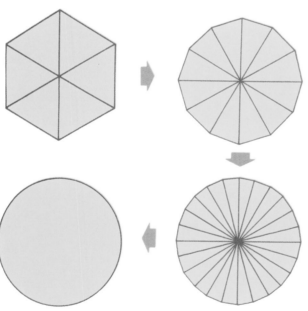

THE STONEMASON CUTS OFF SEGMENTS OF A HEXAGONAL BLOCK, MAKING IT A DODECAGON. THEN MORE SEGMENTS ARE CUT OFF, MAKING IT A TWENTY-FOUR SIDED POLYGON. AN EXACT CIRCLE IS OBTAINED WHEN THE SEGMENTS SO CUT OFF BECOME INFINITESIMALS.

As the number of sides of the polygon increases, its circumference becomes closer to that of the circle. Let me calculate this.

THROUGH THIS METHOD, LIU HUI DETERMINED THAT THE CIRCUMFERENCE OF A 192-SIDED POLYGON WAS 157/50 OF ITS DIAMETER, OR 3.14 TIMES.

20

OVER THE COURSE OF MANY DAYS,
NUMEROUS CIRCLES WERE DRAWN AND
NUMEROUS SECTIONS WERE CUT.
FINALLY, ZU CALCULATED THE VALUE OF π
AS BEING BETWEEN 3.1415926 AND 3.1415927.
ZU WAS THE FIRST PERSON IN THE WORLD TO
GIVE SUCH AN ACCURATE VALUE FOR π.

ZU WAS A VERSATILE SCIENTIST, APPLYING HIS
KNOWLEDGE AND EXPERIENCE TO DIFFERENT FIELDS.
HE EXCELLED IN MACHINE BUILDING, LITERATURE, AND
MUSIC. HE ONCE REBUILT THE SOUTH-POINTING CART
WHICH HAD BEEN LOST DURING HIS TIME. HE ALSO
CREATED METHODS FOR HUSKING RICE AND MILLING
FLOUR DRIVEN BY WATER.

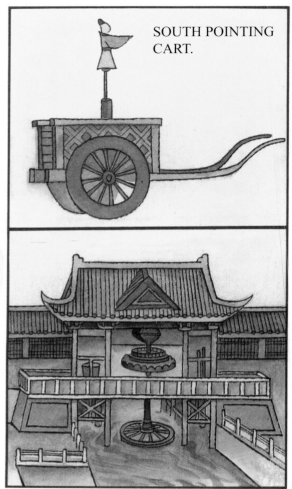

SOUTH POINTING
CART.

FLOUR-MILLING MACHINE
DRIVEN BY WATER POWER.

ZU CHONGZHI DIED IN 500 A.D. HIS SON CARRIED ON HIS LEGACY. TEN YEARS AFTER HIS DEATH,
HIS *DA MING* CALENDAR WAS FINALLY PUBLISHED TO GREAT ACCLAIM.

YI XING AND THE CALENDAR

一行修订历法

YUANDU TEMPLE WAS A TAOIST TEMPLE LOCATED IN CHANG'AN, CAPITAL OF THE TANG DYNASTY. INSIDE THE TEMPLE WERE TENS OF THOUSANDS OF BOOKS. THERE ALSO LIVED A PRIEST NAMED YIN CHONG. AS A YOUNG MAN, ZHANG SUI OFTEN CAME TO ASK YIN CHONG FOR HIS ADVICE.

Teacher, I've finished with the *Canon of Great Mystery*.

You've only spent a couple of days on this complex book. Don't be satisfied with just a smattering of it.

YI XING (683-727 A.D.), ALSO KNOWN AS ZHANG SUI, WAS AN EMINENT MONK AND ASTRONOMER OF THE TANG DYNASTY. HE CREATED THE *DA YAN* CALENDAR WHICH WAS USED FOR NEARLY 1,000 YEARS. HE ALSO CONTRIBUTED TO ASTRONOMICAL OBSERVATIONS, MAKING INSTRUMENTS, AND DIRECTING ASTRONOMICAL AND GEODETIC SURVEYS.

ZHANG SUI SOON BECAME A LEARNED SCHOLAR. WU SANSI, THE NOTORIOUSLY CORRUPT NEPHEW OF THE EMPEROR, SENT ZHANG SUI SEVERAL INVITATIONS AS A WAY OF ATTEMPTING TO GAIN HIS FAVOR.

THUS, IN ORDER NOT TO GET TANGLED UP WITH WU SANSI, ZHANG SUI RESOLUTELY LEFT CHANG'AN FOR MOUNT SONGSHAN IN HENAN TO LIVE THE LIFE OF A MONK.

ZHANG SUI TOOK THE BUDDHIST NAME OF YI XING. HE CONTINUED TO STUDY ASTRONOMY, MATHEMATICS, AND BUDDHIST SUTRAS IN HENAN AND THEN IN ZHEJIANG. HE TRANSLATED AND INTERPRETED MANY KEY BUDDHIST TEXTS AND TEACHINGS.

IN THE YEAR 712, EMPEROR XUANZONG ASCENDED THE THRONE AND ISSUED AN EDICT SEEKING LEARNED SCHOLARS TO HELP ADMINISTER THE COUNTRY. HE URGENTLY REQUESTED ZHANG SUI.

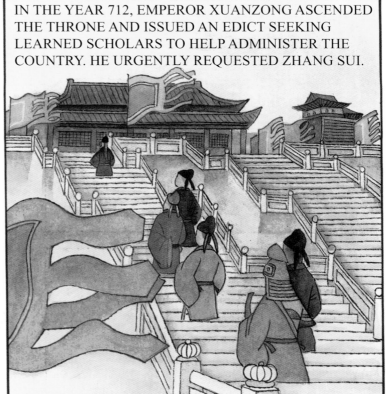

He is now a Buddhist monk! We may not be able to persuade him to come back to the imperial court.

You must persuade him. I need people with his ability and insight.

FORTUNATELY, YI XING WAS PERSUADED TO MEET THE EMPEROR IN CHANG'AN.

25

Your Majesty,
I am Yi Xing.

ACCORDING TO THE CALENDAR, THERE WAS TO BE AN ECLIPSE ON THAT DAY, AND SO ALL THE CIVIL AND MILITARY OFFICIALS ESCORTED THE EMPEROR AND WAITED…

Everyone knows you are learned and wise. I want you to live at the Huanyan Temple here in Chang'an and be my advisor.

Your Majesty, it's not right for a Buddhist monk to be an official at the court. Forgive me.

The sun is setting! Where is the solar eclipse!?

Calm yourself, Sire. The eclipse is coming!

Your Majesty, the calendar is over 50 years old and contains many errors. It needs to be revised.

26

I hereby appoint you in charge of revising the calendar.

We need to rectify and re-record the celestial phenomena. Are there any instruments for making observations?

There is one in the corridor of the back hall.

It's too rusty to be of any use! Who can help me make new instruments?

Liang Lingzan can.

Please bring him here.

After working for four years, Yi Xing and Liang Lingzan invented a new astronomical instrument.

Your Majesty, these rings demonstrate the motion of the sun, the moon, and the stars. Water is used to keep the instrument in balance. This tube is used for observing celestial phenomena and is called the "sighting tube."

The sun doesn't move evenly on the ecliptic. It moves quickly in winter and slowly in summer. It seems wrong that the old calendar divides the year into 24 solar segments.

People say that the stars are fixed, but we have observed over 150 stars and their positions have changed. What causes this?

This shows that the old theory is wrong and the new calendar will correct these errors.

ANOTHER ASTRONOMICAL INSTRUMENT, CALLED A "WATER-OPERATED ARMILLARY SPHERE," WAS LATER BUILT. IT WAS PLACED ON THE TERRACE IN FRONT OF THE PALACE FOR VISITING OFFICIALS.

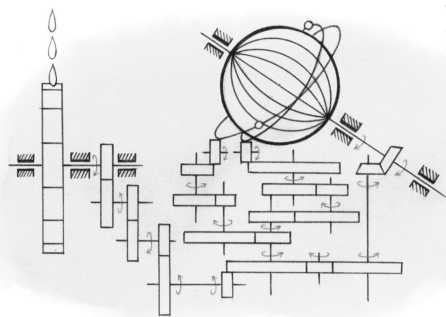

THE NEW WATER-OPERATED ARMILLARY SPHERE WAS BUILT FOLLOWING THE ORIGINAL SPHERE MADE BY ZHANG HENG OF THE EASTERN HAN DYNASTY. THE NEW SPHERE ADDED TWO RINGS WHICH REPRESENTED THE MOTION OF THE SUN AND MOON IN RELATION TO THE SKY. THE RING CONTAINING THE SUN MAKES AN EASTWARD CIRCUIT OF THE CELESTIAL GLOBE EVERY 365 DAYS, WHILE THE RING CONTAINING THE MOON MAKES A CIRCUIT EVERY 29 DAYS. THE GLOBE ITSELF MAKES A COMPLETE REVOLUTION ONCE A DAY. IN THIS WAY THE CYCLE OF MOTION FOR THE SUN, MOON, AND THE EARTH IS SHOWN.

Master Yi Xing, we have accumulated considerable data and may start to make a new calendar.

Not yet. The figures must be checked and verified first.

IN 724, A LARGE-SCALE PROJECT BEGAN.

You go to the four corners of Henan to take measurements. Please take accurate figures.

I will.

The ancient records say that a thousand li from north to south results in a tolerance of one *cun* between the shadows of bamboo poles. According to this, the earth can be measured.

Is this theory correct? No one has proved it. We must try to prove it ourselves.

YI XING SENT 12 TEAMS TO ALL PARTS OF THE EMPIRE. THEY WERE TO TAKE MEASUREMENTS, WITH HENAN AS THE CENTER. THE TEAMS WERE SUPPOSED TO MEASURE THE LENGTH OF THE SHADOWN OF AN EIGHT-CHI-LONG BAMBOO POLE AT NOON IN THE FOUR DAYS OF THE SPRING EQUINOX (4TH SOLAR TERM), SUMMER SOLSTICE (10TH SOLAR TERM), AUTUMNAL EQUINOX (16TH SOLAR TERM), AND THE WINTER SOLSTICE (22ND SOLAR TERM). ALSO MEASURED WAS THE EXACT DURATION OF DAY AND NIGHT.

Master, these are the figures in the four counties of Henan.

Let me have a look.

According to these figures, every 277 li results in one *cun* of difference in shadow.

30

YI XING CALCULATED THE MERIDIAN AS 82 MILES ON THE BASIS OF THE FIGURES. EVEN IF IT WAS NOT A PRECISE CALCULATION COMPARED WITH THE MODERN FIGURE OF 70 MILES, IT WAS THE FIRST TIME MAN HAD CALCULATED THE MERIDIAN.

YI XING INVENTED A SPECIAL INSTRUMENT FOR MEASURING THE LENGTH OF THE MERIDIAN ARC.

SOON AFTER THE COMPLETION OF THE *DA YAN* CALENDAR, HOWEVER, YI XING FELL ILL AND COULD NO LONGER LEAVE THE HUAYAN TEMPLE. HE DIED THERE A MONTH LATER, AT AGE 45.

WHEN COMPARED WITH ITS PREDECESSORS, THE *DA YAN* CALENDAR WAS MORE ACCURATE AND BETTER ORGANIZED. IT WAS ONE OF THE FINEST CALENDARS IN ANCIENT CHINA, AND WAS STILL IN USE UP TO THE SIXTEENTH CENTURY.

THE TRAVELS OF XU XIAKE

徐霞客游记

Confucius says: "A gentleman is not bitter even though his deeds go unrecognized."

Eh? What's that you're reading?

The "Illustrated Classic of Mountains and Rivers!?"

You are reading such an inelegant work instead of Confucius?!

XU XIAKE (1586-1641), ORIGINALLY NAMED XU HONGZU, WAS A GEOGRAPHER DURING THE LATE MING DYNASTY. BEGINNING FROM AGE 22 TO THE AGE OF 56, XU TRAVELED ALL ACROSS CHINA AND INVESTIGATED AND RECORDED VARIOUS DETAILS OF THE COUNTRYSIDE, ITS LANDFORMS, FLORA, FAUNA, AND GEOGRAPHY. HIS WORK, COMPILED AS *THE TRAVELS OF XU XIAKE*, HAS BROUGHT A WEALTH OF INFORMATION ON CHINA'S GEOGRAPHY TO FUTURE GENERATIONS.

XU'S FAMILY HAD A LIBRARY. EVERY DAY WHEN HE CAME BACK FROM SCHOOL HE BURIED HIMSELF IN HISTORY BOOKS.

IN 1607, AT THE AGE OF 22, XU GOT MARRIED, BUT HE WAS STILL EAGER TO TRAVEL.

I've made this cap for you to take on your trip.

Thank you, Mother.

Please be careful, and take care of yourself.

I will.

Come back soon or we will worry.

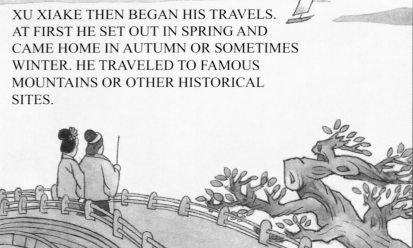

XU XIAKE THEN BEGAN HIS TRAVELS. AT FIRST HE SET OUT IN SPRING AND CAME HOME IN AUTUMN OR SOMETIMES WINTER. HE TRAVELED TO FAMOUS MOUNTAINS OR OTHER HISTORICAL SITES.

What a brave man!

That's Xu Xiake. As for mountain climbing, even I can't match him.

What a wonderful view. Incredible!

HE STAYED AT AN INN FOR THE NIGHT.

Your feet must be tired!

First I must finish writing down everything I saw today.

IN 1613, XU XIAKE, TOGETHER WITH HIS SERVANTS, CAME TO YANDANG MOUNTAIN IN ZHEJIANG.

The waterfall is so loud!

Does the Dragon King spit out the water?

This is called the Dalongjiu waterfall. It starts from a lake on top of Yandang Mountain. Let's find it.

Shouldn't we turn back?

It's too dangerous. Where is the lake?

Look! There may be a path under the cliff. Lower me into the gully.

You're crazy! You'll be killed if you fall.

There's no path. Where on earth is the lake?

Be careful!

There's nothing here. Pull me up.

That was too close!

How unlucky! There's no lake and you almost fell to your death!

It's natural to run into risks when making explorations.

38

IN 1616, XU XIAKE CLIMBED MOUNT HUANGSHAN.

How can we get to the summit?

The snow has covered the mountain passes. You can't get to the top.

We'll be careful. Please show us the way.

Just go eastward along the steps, but be careful!

Ah! The steps are covered with ice!

It's too slippery!

I'll poke holes in the ice. You just follow my steps.

40

WITH HIS INCREASED KNOWLEDGE, XU BEGAN TO PROBE INTO THE LAWS OF NATURE AND DOCUMENTED MANY SCIENTIFIC OBSERVATIONS.

IN 1628 HE CAME TO FUJIAN PROVINCE AND INVESTIGATED THE JIANXI AND NINGYANG RIVERS.

XU WONDERED WHY THE TWO RIVERS STARTED AT THE SAME ELEVATION, BUT THE FLOW OF THE CURRENT OF THE NINGYANG RIVER WAS TEN TIMES THAT OF THE JIANXI RIVER. BY INVESTIGATING FUTHER, HE DISCOVERED THE REASON: THE JIANXI RIVER MEANDERS FOR 250 MILES BEFORE REACHING THE SEA, WHILE THE NINGYANG TRAVELS ONLY 93 MILES. XU OBSERVED THAT THE SHORTER THE RIVER, THE MORE RAPID THE CURRENT.

IN 1632, XU AGAIN CLIMBED YANDANG MOUNTAIN VIA ANOTHER PATH AND FINALLY FOUND THE LAKE. HE DISCOVERED THAT WHILE THE LAKE PRODUCED TWO RIVERS, IT WAS NOT THE SOURCE OF THE WATERFALL, THUS DISPROVING THE PREVIOUS THEORY.

IN 1636 XU WAS 51 YEARS OLD. HE PREPARED FOR A LONG TRIP TO SOUTHWEST CHINA.

Dad, it's too far. Don't go.

You've traveled so much already. Take a rest and enjoy life.

I'm getting old and must make the best use of my time.

A MONK NAMED JINGWEN WAS GOING ON A RELIGIOUS PILGRIMAGE AND WANTED TO JOIN XU.

Master Xu, may I accompany you?

Of course. Welcome aboard.

FOUR MONTHS LATER THEY REACHED XINTANG, HUNAN PROVINCE.

Stop!

Bandits!

Run!

It's safe here.

We've lost everything!

Don't lose faith. All our material possessions can be replaced.

Let's not get disheartened. I say we keep going.

Look at that view!

SOON, THEY REACHED QIYANG. SUDDENLY, INCREDIBLE ROCK FORMATIONS BEGAN TO APPEAR ON BOTH SIDES OF THE RIVER. THIS TYPE OF FORMATION IN CHINA IS KNOWN AS "KARST," WHICH RESULTS FROM THE EROSION OF WATER ON LIMESTONE. XU WAS THE FIRST TO INVESTIGATE KARST TOPOGRAPHY IN SOUTHWEST CHINA.

Monsters, eh? Have you seen them?

If there are monsters, I'd like to meet them.

How far do we have to go?

There is a cave nearby, but we can't go inside. There are monsters living there!

Be careful! And watch your step!

It's like a maze in here. I've never seen anything like it before!

It must have been made by the immortals!

Now I see. The sediment carried in water forms the stone pillars. It must be incredibly old!

44

You've been gone so long we feared you were captured by monsters!

We're fine. What's happening?

Master Xu! Come quickly! Master Jingwen is very ill!

Master Xu, I'm dying. Please take this sutra and present it to the Buddha.

I'll do my best.

SHORTLY THEREAFTER, JINGWEN DIED. XU XIAKE WAS VERY SAD.

LATER, XU'S LONG TIME SERVANTS FLED WITH HIS BELONGINGS.

BUT XU WAS NEVER DEJECTED, AND SAID, "AS LONG AS MY LEGS CAN MOVE, I'LL NEVER STOP TRAVELING!"
HE INVESTIGATED MORE THAN A HUNDRED CAVES AND GROTTOES AND RECORDED AN IMMEASURABLE QUANTITY OF INFORMATION DURING THE REMAINDER OF HIS JOURNEY.

XU IDENTIFIED THE SOURCES OF MANY LAKES, RIVERS, AND STREAMS, AND ALSO RESEARCHED THE PHENOMENA OF HOT SPRINGS AND TERRESTRIAL HEAT.

Ah! I feel completely relaxed!

XU'S TRIP TO SOUTHWEST CHINA LASTED FOUR YEARS. UPON HIS RETURN HOME, HE FELL ILL AND DIED IN 1641.

HIS WRITINGS, GATHERED OVER A LIFETIME OF TRAVELS, WERE COMPILED BY LATER GENERATIONS AND PUBLISHED AS *THE TRAVELS OF XU XIAKE*. XU'S BOOK IS EQUALLY VALUABLE FOR ITS CONTRIBUTION TO CHINESE LITERATURE AS WELL AS FOR ITS SCIENTIFIC OBSERVATIONS, WHICH WERE HUNDREDS OF YEARS AHEAD OF OTHER ACCOUNTS PUBLISHED IN THE WEST.